Comptroller of the Currency
Administrator of National Banks

Leveraged Lending

Comptroller's Handbook

February 2008

A

Assets

Leveraged Lending   Table of Contents

Leveraged Lending   Introduction

This booklet describes the fundamentals of leveraged finance. The booklet summarizes leveraged lending risks, discusses how a bank can prudently manage these risks, and incorporates previous OCC guidance on the subject. One of a series of specialized lending booklets of the Comptroller's Handbook, "Leveraged Lending" supplements the general guidance in the "Loan Portfolio Management" and "Commercial Lending" booklets.

Overview

Leveraged lending is a type of corporate finance used for mergers and acquisitions, business recapitalization and refinancing, equity buyouts, and business or product line build-outs and expansions. It is used to increase shareholder returns and to monetize perceived "enterprise value" or other intangibles. In this type of transaction, debt is commonly used as an alternative to equity when financing business expansions and acquisitions. It can serve to support business growth and increase returns to investors by financing business operations that generate incremental profits against a fixed equity investment. While it is more prevalent in certain industries and with larger companies, banks provide leveraged financing to a variety of borrowers for a variety of reasons.

Institutions participate in leveraged lending activities on a number of levels. In addition to providing senior financing, they extend or arrange credit on a subordinated basis (mezzanine financing), and can provide short-term, or "bridge," financing to expedite the syndication process. Institutions and their affiliates also may take equity positions in leveraged companies with direct investments through affiliated securities firms, small business investment companies (SBICs), and venture capital companies; or they may take equity interests through warrants and other equity "kickers" received as part of a financing package. Institutions also may invest in leveraged loan funds managed by investment banking companies or other third parties.

Although leveraged financing is more prevalent in large banks, it can be found in banks of all sizes. Large banks increasingly follow an "originate-to-distribute" model with respect to large loans. This model, whereby a bank or group of banks arrange, underwrite, and then market all or some portion of the loan facilities to third-party investors, allows the banks to earn fees while limiting their overall exposure to the borrower. This can be especially important in certain leveraged lending transactions, such as those financing corporate buyouts, when the amount of the total credit facility can be quite large. Smaller banks participate in the leveraged loan market by either purchasing participations in these large corporate loans or by making direct extensions to smaller companies.

Leveraged Lending Defined

Numerous definitions of leveraged lending exist throughout the financial services industry. Depending upon the source, definitions commonly contain one or more of the following conditions:

- Proceeds used for buyouts, acquisition, and recapitalization.

- Transaction results in a substantial increase in borrower's leverage ratio. Industry benchmarks include a twofold increase in the borrower's liabilities, resulting in a balance sheet leverage ratio (total liabilities/total assets) higher than 50 percent, or an increase in the balance sheet leverage ratio more than 75 percent. Other benchmarks include increasing the borrower's operating leverage ratios [total debt/ EBITDA (earnings before interest, taxes, depreciation, and amortization) or senior debt/EBITDA] above defined levels such as above 4.0X EBITDA or 3.0X EBITDA, respectively.

- Transactions designated as a highly leveraged transaction (HLT) by the syndication agent.

- Borrower rated as a non-investment-grade company with a high debt to net worth ratio.

- Loan pricing indicates a non-investment-grade company. This generally consists of some spread over LIBOR (London Interbank Offered Rate) that fluctuates as a function of market conditions.

The OCC broadly considers a leveraged loan to be a transaction where the borrower's post-financing leverage, when measured by debt-to-assets, debt-to-equity, cash flow-to-total debt, or other such standards unique to particular industries, significantly exceeds industry norms for leverage.

Banks engaging in this type of activity should define leveraged lending within their lending policy. Examiners should expect the bank's definition to clearly describe the purpose and financial characteristics common in these transactions.

Leveraged Lending and the Syndicated Loan Market

The size and complexity of characteristics inherent in many leveraged transactions require funding through the syndicated loan market. Loan syndications offer many advantages to borrowers and lenders.

Syndicated loans allow borrowers to access a larger pool of capital than any one single lender may be prepared to make available and allow the originating lender the opportunity to provide greater customization than with traditional bilateral relationship-based loans. Syndicated loans are simpler for borrowers and lenders to arrange and less costly than borrowing the same amount from a number of lenders through traditional bilateral loan underwritings. Moreover, there is an active secondary market, and credit ratings for many leveraged loans, which permit more effective credit portfolio management activities. Finally, syndicated loans provide borrowers a more complete array of financing and relationship-based options.

Syndication of leveraged loans allows originating lenders to serve client needs while at the same time ensuring appropriate risk diversification in their permanent loan portfolios. Large bank agents and participants can also capitalize on a lucrative array of fee income from arranging and underwriting the transaction as well as ancillary fee income associated with other banking services provided to the borrower. Corporate borrowers often require banks to participate in their credit facilities before purchasing other corporate treasury products. Participating in a syndicate may be attractive to smaller lenders as well, since it allows them to lend to larger borrowers than their smaller balance sheets would allow in the case of bilateral loans. A syndicate

---

may be valuable in workouts as it can provide for a coordinated means of dealing with a problem borrowing situation, as opposed to an expensive and complex "free for all" of competing claims. However, syndicate membership may also contain numerous nonbank entities, including private equity groups, hedge funds, and investment conduits. These organizations may have risk appetites, investment strategies, and workout motivations that differ significantly from bank members, complicating the workout process.

Distributions and Bridge Financing

Asset sales, participations, syndication, and other means of distribution are critical elements in the growth of leveraged financing. Distributions most often consist of "club" arrangements, "best effort" syndications, and "underwritten" deals.

"Club" deals usually consist of smaller credits, which the arranger markets to a small group of relationship lenders. A club deal may not be governed by a single loan agreement; however, participating lenders usually have very similar, if not identical, terms. "Best efforts" and "underwritten" syndications support larger transaction sizes. In a best effort syndication deal, the underwriter agrees to use all efforts to sell as much of the loan as possible. However, if the underwriter is unable to sell the entire amount of the loan, they are not responsible for funding any unsold portions. Such deals may include flex language that provides for pricing changes if the credit markets or borrower's conditions change to facilitate the arranger gaining market acceptance for the credit. An "underwritten" deal, on the other hand, is one in which the arranger commits to the borrower the entire loan amount before syndication of the loan. If the arranger cannot fully syndicate the loan, it must hold the unsold portion, which exposes it to price risk.

Banks can also provide temporary bridge financing during the syndication period to be repaid through subsequent debt or equity offerings. Risk increases with this activity as the source of repayment is dependent on investor appetite, liquidity, and market demand, which may significantly change during this period. In addition to providing temporary financing for the borrower's debt, syndicating institutions may bridge the equity level of the transaction until the ownership group is finalized. Because national banks have statutory restrictions against owning equity, equity bridges are typically provided by the parent holding company or securities affiliate. Equity bridges carry additional risk, including the heavy reliance on sponsors to sell equity to limited partners and other investors, potential contractual limits on sales rights, a limited secondary private equity market, and the questionable ability to place the equity if the deal sponsor has tried and failed.

Risks Associated with Leveraged Lending

For purposes of the OCC's discussion of risk, examiners assess banking risk relative to its impact on capital and earnings. From a supervisory perspective, risk is the potential that events, expected or unanticipated, may have an adverse impact on the bank's capital and earnings. The OCC has defined nine categories of risk for bank supervision purposes. These risks are credit, interest rate, liquidity, price, foreign exchange, transaction, compliance, strategic, and reputation. These categories are not mutually exclusive; any product or service may expose a bank to multiple risks. For analysis and discussion purposes, however, the OCC identifies and assesses the risks separately. The primary risks associated with leveraged lending are credit, price, liquidity, reputation, compliance, and strategic.

Credit Risk

Credit risk is the current and prospective risk to earnings or capital arising from a borrower's failure to meet the terms of any contract with a bank or otherwise to perform as agreed. Credit risk is found in all activities where success depends on counterparty, issuer, or borrower performance. It arises any time bank funds are extended, committed, invested, or otherwise exposed through actual or implied contractual agreements, whether reflected on or off the balance sheet.

High debt levels increase the risk of default. Leveraged borrowers' higher debt levels relative to their equity, income, or cash flow make it more difficult for the borrower to withstand adverse economic conditions or business plan variances, to take advantage of new business opportunities, or to make necessary capital expenditures.

The primary source of repayment in all leveraged transactions is the borrower's ability to generate a satisfactory level of cash flows. Secondary sources of repayment include refinancing, recapitalizing, or restructuring of debt through the sale or disposal of the company assets or stock. When the borrower's use of increased debt does not generate sufficient cash flows or asset values, both primary and secondary repayment sources may be quickly and seriously impaired.

Leveraged transactions, in general, are characterized by a high level of debt, increased volatility of corporate earnings and cash flow, and limited avenues of secondary support. In addition to these more general factors, other features in leveraged lending activities heighten credit risk, and warrant more intensive risk analysis, monitoring, and management. These factors include:

- **Debt Structures and Collateral.** Leveraged loans are typically structured with a revolving credit facility and several term loan tranches with successively longer repayment terms. The revolving debt portion may be secured by a traditional borrowing base of working assets, with the term tranches collateralized by available business assets and stock. Leveraged transactions are often characterized by a reliance on enterprise values and a financing gap between the value of the collateralized assets and the amount of the loan. As overall debt levels increase, the borrower's needs exceed conventional collateral advance formulas. In such cases, working capital assets will be used to secure long-term debt, fixed asset collateral will secure revolving facilities, and, as a result of these two events, the financing gap, that is, the amount of the loan not supported by collateral, may widen. These practices dilute the lender's overall collateral protection. In many cases, these structured transactions contain cross-collateralization and cross-default provisions, which further dilute collateral protection for each component.

- **Repayment Terms.** Longer tenors, deferred or back-ended principal amortization, and single payment notes are increasingly common in leveraged lending structures. In many cases, the economic benefit of the asset or transaction financed with increased leverage will not be immediately realized by the borrower. As a result, principal repayment requirements are deferred or otherwise set to coincide with the realization of expected repayment sources. This often occurs when lenders finance capital intensive or expanding businesses that must invest significant amounts of cash to fund long-term capital investments. It also occurs when lenders finance merger and acquisition activities, and in transactions where asset prices and business valuations are unproven or increasing relative to historical income and cash generation capability. Longer tenors can be appropriate when they are coordinated with the economic use and value of the asset or transaction financed, as well as with the level and timing of expected cash flows. However, they are not appropriate when used to mask credit weaknesses related to the borrower, liberalize repayment terms for projects that have been "over-financed," or provide permanent capital.

- **Reliance on Refinancing or Recapitalization.** Lending and equity markets can be volatile. When markets are liquid, reflecting strong demand by banks and institutional investors for loan assets, and attractive conditions for firms to issue equity, many borrowers negotiate deal structures that rely on loan refinancing or a capital issuance as the primary repayment source. Often, there is no clearly defined or realistic alternative source of repayment. Loan arrangements that rely on refinancing or equity issuance in the capital markets carry the added element of market risk. Market liquidity and receptiveness can dissipate quickly for reasons beyond the control of the lender or borrower and rapidly elevate risk.

- **Reliance on "Enterprise Value" and "Airballs."** Enterprise value, which is basically the estimated value of the borrower as a going concern, is typically used by banks to support leveraged lending arrangements when committed amounts exceed the borrower's underlying tangible asset values. Historically, these under-collateralized positions, or "airballs," have included accelerated or prioritized repayment, or have been held by subordinated lenders. Enterprise values can be highly volatile as they are subject to influences both within and beyond the control of the parties (e.g., interest rates, conditions in the industry, economy, or capital markets). Valuations depend on management's ability to achieve revenue and expense projections, and are difficult to fully support. Moreover, enterprise value is especially susceptible to decline when most needed by the lender, e.g., in problem situations or in an economic downturn.

- **Interdependent Repayment Sources.** Leveraged loans are often underwritten with collateral liquidation, asset sales, refinancing, or recapitalization as secondary sources of repayment. The value of such secondary sources is often directly linked to the strength of cash flow. Hence, their value may diminish in tandem with cash flow, thus increasing the risk of loss in the event of default. Risk is increased even further when both primary and secondary repayment sources depend on achieving performance levels (sales, income, cash flows, asset values, etc.) above those demonstrated historically.

- **Reliance on Equity Sponsors and Agent Banks.** Some banks participate in leveraged loan transactions based on the strength and reputation of equity sponsors. They believe that major equity sponsors will support their transactions (e.g., provide additional equity, halt dividends, further subordinate rights to senior lenders) in order to protect their investments and reputations. Lenders sometimes place too much reliance on this informal support. The sponsor's primary obligation is to support its investors by enhancing profits, cash flow, and, ultimately, the value of the company. Its ability to provide additional support is limited by the firm's legal charter, its financial capacity, and its economic incentive to support the company.

Price Risk

Price risk is the current and prospective risk to earnings or capital arising from changes in the value of traded portfolios of financial instruments. This risk arises from market making, dealing, and position-taking in interest rate, foreign exchange, and equity and commodities markets.

Price risk associated with underwriting syndicated leveraged loans can be high because changes in investor appetite can impair the originator's ability to sell down positions as planned. Originators of leveraged loans commit credit terms to borrowers, and then must syndicate the loans with those terms to the investor community.

Occasionally, investor appetite for credit risk can suddenly change, sometimes sharply, and originators find that they cannot syndicate at acceptable prices the loans held in their pipeline. When this happens, originators can try to renegotiate terms with the borrower. However, except in unusual circumstances, borrowers or their financial sponsors have limited incentive to make changes to credit terms that have become very favorable in light of the changes in market conditions. Alternatively, originators can sell the assets at a loss, hold the "stuck" loans in a held-for-sale account, or reassess their planned portfolio hold level.

There are a number of unique accounting issues with respect to accounting for syndicated loans. Refer to Appendix C, "Accounting for Leveraged Lending," for more detailed information.

Liquidity Risk

Liquidity risk is the current and prospective risk to earnings or capital arising from a bank's inability to meet its obligations when they come due without incurring unacceptable losses. Liquidity risk includes the inability to manage unplanned decreases or changes in funding sources. Liquidity risk also arises from a bank's failure to recognize or address changes in market conditions that affect the ability to liquidate assets quickly and with minimal loss in value.

Changes in investor appetite and market volatility can adversely affect the liquidity of a bank's leveraged lending portfolio. As noted above, such changes can result in a bank's need to fund (hold) a larger amount of the loan than originally planned or distribute at a reduced price. Hold limits for all members in a syndicate group, regardless of role, can change from that originally planned. In addition, the ability to liquidate portions of the portfolio to meet other funding requirements or take advantage of other opportunities can be affected significantly by the market's demand for this asset class.

Compliance Risk

Compliance risk is the current and prospective risk to earnings or capital arising from violations of, or non-compliance with, laws, rules, regulations, prescribed practices, or ethical standards. Compliance risk also arises in situations where the laws or rules governing certain bank products or activities of the bank's clients may be ambiguous or untested. This risk exposes the institution to possible fines, civil money penalties, payment of damages, and the voiding of contracts. Compliance risk can lead to a diminished reputation, reduced franchise value, limited business opportunities, lessened expansion potential, and lack of contract enforceability.

Many larger banks originate, arrange and sell leveraged loans, in various capacities, through their syndication activities. Failure to meet the contractual and fiduciary responsibilities arising from these legal arrangements exposes banks to substantial penalties and civil liability.

Reputation Risk

Reputation risk is the current and prospective risk to earnings or capital arising from negative public opinion. This risk affects the institution's ability to establish new relationships or services, or continue servicing existing relationships. This risk can expose the institution to litigation, financial loss, or damage to its reputation. Reputation risk exposure is present throughout the organization and includes the responsibility to exercise an abundance of caution in dealing with its customers and community. This risk is present in such activities as asset management and agency transactions.

Leveraged loans are often syndicated throughout the institutional market due to their size and risk characteristics. A bank's failure to meet its moral, legal or fiduciary responsibilities in implementing these activities can damage its reputation and impair its ability to compete successfully in this business line.

Leveraged loans may also include the characteristics of a complex structured finance transaction. The activities associated with these transactions, as fully discussed in OCC Bulletin 2007-1, typically involve the structuring of cash flows and the allocation of risk among borrowers and investors to meet the specific objectives of the customer in more efficient ways. They often involve professionals from multiple disciplines within a financial institution and may be associated with the creation or use of one or more special purpose entities designed to address the economic, legal, tax, or accounting objectives of the customer. Although in the vast majority of cases, structured finance products and the roles played by banks with respect to these products serve legitimate business purposes of customers, banks may be exposed to substantial reputation and legal risks if they enter into transactions without sufficient due diligence, oversight, and internal controls.

Strategic Risk

Strategic risk is the current and prospective impact on earnings or capital arising from adverse business decisions, improper implementation of a decision, or lack of responsiveness to industry changes. This risk is a function of the compatibility of an organization's strategic goals, the business strategies developed to achieve those goals, the resources deployed against these goals, and the quality of implementation. The resources needed to carry out business strategies are both tangible and intangible. This includes communication channels, operating systems, delivery networks, and managerial capacities. The organization's internal characteristics must be evaluated against the impact of economic, technological, competitive, regulatory and environmental changes.

A bank's decision to be involved in leveraged lending requires advanced account and portfolio management practices. Failure of the board of directors and bank management to provide a commensurate level of oversight and supervision may expose the bank to significant exposure from the interrelationship of the risk factors discussed above and from the conflicts of interest arising from the multiple roles in which the institution or its affiliates may be involved.

Risk Management Guidelines and Controls

All banks engaging in leveraged lending activities should state in writing their risk objectives, underwriting standards, and controls as part of their overall credit risk management process and policies. The lack of robust risk management processes and controls in banks with significant leveraged lending activities is an unsafe and unsound banking practice. The bank's loan policies should avoid compromising sound banking practices in an effort to broaden market share or generate substantial fees.

Loan Policy

A bank's board of directors should adopt formal written policies which specifically address:

- The definition of leveraged lending and risk objectives.
- Loan approval requirements that require sufficient senior level oversight.
- Responsibilities regarding the establishment of underwriting standards, distribution practices, and credit risk management controls.
- Pricing policies that ensure a prudent tradeoff between risk and return.
- The requirement for action plans whenever cash flow, asset sale proceeds, or collateral values decline significantly from projections. Action plans should include remedial initiatives and triggers for risk rating changes, changes to accrual status, and loss recognition.

Underwriting Standards

The following issues should be addressed either in the loan policies or specific underwriting guidelines:
- Appropriate loan structures.
- Amortization requirements of term loans.
- Collateral requirements, including acceptable types of collateral, loan-to-value limits, collateral margins, and appropriate valuation methodologies.
- Covenant requirements, particularly minimum interest and fixed charge coverage and maximum leverage ratios.

- How enterprise values and other intangible business values may be used, along with acceptable methodologies, and frequency and independence of assessment reviews.
- Minimum documentation requirements for appraisals and valuations, including enterprise values and other intangibles.
- Acceptable fixed charge coverage ratios and standards for calculation.
- Measures of debt repayment capacity that reflect a borrower's ability to repay debt without undue reliance on refinancing.
- For loans originated -for sale, the degree to which underwriting standards are permitted by policy to deviate from underwriting standard for loans originated for portfolio or investment.

Policies and Procedures on Loan Acquisition and Distribution

Market disruption can impede the ability of an agent (originating) bank to consummate syndications or otherwise sell down loan exposures. As a result, the bank, as agent, may have to hold higher-than-planned exposure levels. Banks should develop procedures for defining and managing distribution fails, which are generally defined as an inability to sell down the exposure within a reasonable distribution period (generally 90 days).

Agent banks should clearly define their hold level before syndication efforts begin in accordance with accounting guidance. Generally accepted accounting principles require that loans originated with the intent to sell, with the exception of those loans for which the institution has elected to account at fair value under the fair value option, must be carried on the bank's books at the lower of cost or market (LOCOM). In addition, loans transferred to the "Held for Investment" portfolio that were originated with the intent to sell must be transferred at LOCOM. Methodologies used by the bank to establish carrying and transfer values should be closely reviewed for compliance with accounting guidance and reasonableness.

Institutions should adopt formal policies and procedures addressing the distribution and acquisition of leveraged financing transactions. Policies should include:

- Procedures for defining, managing, and accounting for distribution fails.
- Identification of any sales made with recourse and procedures for fully reflecting the risk of any such sales.
- A process to ensure that purchasers are provided with timely, current financial information.
- A process to determine the portion of a transaction to be held in the portfolio and the portion to be held for sale.
- Procedures and management information systems (MIS) to identify, control, and monitor syndication pipeline exposure.
- Limits on the length of time transactions can be held in the held-for-sale account and policies for handling items that exceed those limits.
- Reasonable and consistently applied methodologies for determining market values and prompt recognition of losses for loans classified as held-for-sale in accordance with generally accepted accounting principles.
- Procedural safeguards to prevent conflicts of interest for both bank and affiliated securities firms.
- Procedures defining controls, independence, and limits on an affiliate's equity interests in leveraged transactions.

Setting Concentration Limits

Leveraged finance and other loan portfolios with above-average default probabilities tend to behave similarly during an economic or sectoral downturn. Consequently, banks should take steps to avoid undue concentrations by setting limits consistent with their appetite for risk and their financial capacity. Banks should ensure that they monitor and control as separate risk concentrations those loan segments most vulnerable to default. For example, banks should consider identifying concentrations by:
- The degree of leverage in the transaction.
- The bank's internal risk grade.
- Industry or other factors that the bank determines are correlated with an above-average default probability.

In addition, sub-limits may be appropriate by collateral type, loan purpose, secondary source of repayment, and sponsor relationships. Banks should also establish limits for the aggregate number of policy exceptions.

Credit Analysis

Effective management of leveraged financing risk is highly dependent on the quality of analysis during the approval process and after the loan is funded. At a minimum, analysis of leveraged financing transactions should ensure that:

- Cash flow analysis adequately supports a borrower's ability to repay debt based on actual and projected cash flows, and is well documented and supported.
- Analysis does not rely on overly optimistic or unsubstantiated projections of sales, margins, and merger and acquisition synergies.
- Projections provide an adequate margin for unanticipated merger-related integration costs.
- Projections are appropriately stress tested for one or multiple downside scenarios.
- Transactions are reviewed at least quarterly to determine variance from financial plans, the risk implications thereof, and the accuracy of risk ratings and accrual status.
- Collateral and "enterprise" valuations are derived with a proper degree of independence and consider potential value erosion.
- Collateral liquidation and asset sale estimates are conservative.
- Potential collateral shortfalls are identified and factored into risk rating, accrual, and allowance for loan and lease loss decisions.
- Contingency plans anticipate changing conditions in debt or equity markets when exposures rely on refinancing or re-capitalization.
- The borrower is adequately protected from interest rate and foreign exchange risks.

Risk Identification System

Banks need thoroughly articulated policies that specify requirements and criteria for risk rating transactions, identifying loan impairment, and recognizing losses. Such specificity is critical for maintaining the integrity of an institution's risk management system. The internal rating systems of banks materially involved in leveraged lending should integrate both the probability of default and loss given default in their ratings to ensure that the risk of the borrower and the risk of the transaction structure itself are clearly evaluated.

This is particularly important for leveraged finance transaction structures, which can result in large losses upon default.

Problem Loan Management

Banks should formulate individual action plans with clear and quantifiable objectives and timeframes for adversely rated and other high-risk borrowers whose operating performance departs significantly from planned cash flows, asset sales, collateral values, or other important targets. Actions may include working with the borrower for an orderly resolution while preserving the bank's interests, sale of the loan in the secondary market, and liquidation. Examiners and bankers need to ensure problem credits are reviewed regularly for risk rating accuracy, accrual status, recognition of impairment through specific allocations, and charge-offs.

Reports on Leveraged Finance Transactions

Higher risk credits, including leveraged finance transactions, require frequent monitoring by banking organizations. Bank management and the board of directors should receive comprehensive reports about the characteristics and trends in such exposures, generally at least quarterly. These reports should include at a minimum:
- Total exposure and segment exposures, including subordinated debt and equity holdings, compared to established limits.
- Risk rating distribution and migration data.
- Portfolio performance — noncompliance with covenants, restructured loans, delinquencies, non-performing assets, impaired loans, and charge-offs.
- Compliance with internal procedures and the aggregate level of exceptions to policy and underwriting standards.

Banks with significant exposure levels to higher-risk credits should consider additional reports covering:

- Collateral composition of the portfolio, e.g., percentages supported by working assets, fixed assets, intangibles, blanket liens, and stock of the borrower's operating subsidiaries.
- Unsecured, partially secured, or "airball" exposures, including potential collateral shortfalls caused by defaults that trigger pari passu collateral treatment for all lender classes.
- Absolute amount and percentage of the portfolio dependent on refinancing, recapitalization, asset sales, and enterprise value.
- Absolute amounts and percentages of scheduled and actual annual portfolio amortizations.
- Secondary market pricing data and trading volume for loans in the portfolio when available.
- Loan performance and exposure by individual sponsor.

Internal Reviews on Leveraged Credits

Banks engaged in leveraged finance need to ensure that their internal review function is appropriately staffed to provide timely and independent assessments of leveraged credits. Reviews should evaluate risk rating integrity, valuation methodologies, and the quality of risk management. Because of the volatile nature of this type of lending, portfolio reviews should be conducted on at least an annual basis. For many institutions, the risk characteristics of the leveraged portfolio, such as high reliance on enterprise value, concentrations, and adverse risk rating trends or portfolio performance, will warrant more frequent reviews.

Allowance for Loan and Lease Losses

Banks with held for investment leveraged loans need to ensure that the risks are fully incorporated in the allowance for loan and lease losses and capital adequacy analyses. For allowance purposes, leverage exposures should be taken into account either through analysis of the estimated credit losses from the discrete portfolio or as part of an overall analysis of the portfolio using the institution's internal risk grades or other factors. At the transaction level, exposures heavily reliant on enterprise value as a secondary source of repayment require special evaluation to determine the need for, and adequacy of, specific allocations as these values can be highly volatile and difficult to fully support.

When banks hold significantly greater exposures than originally intended, bankers and examiners must evaluate their effect on overall portfolio risk levels, and the adequacy of capital and the allowance for loan and lease losses.

Refer to Appendix C, "Accounting for Leveraged Lending," for additional discussion on the accounting implications.

Policies on Purchasing Participations in Leveraged Loans

As outlined in OCC Banking Circular 181, banks purchasing participations and assignments in leveraged loan arrangements must make a thorough, independent evaluation of the transaction and the risks involved before committing any funds. They should apply the same standards of prudence, credit assessment and approval criteria, and "in-house" limits that would be employed if the purchasing organization were originating the loan. At a minimum, policies should include the following requirements:

- Obtaining and independently analyzing full credit information both before the participation is purchased and on a timely basis thereafter.
- Obtaining from the lead lender copies of all executed and proposed loan documents, legal opinions, title insurance policies, UCC searches, and other relevant documents.
- Carefully monitoring the borrower's performance throughout the life of the loan.
- Establishing appropriate risk management guidelines.

Evaluating the Borrower in a Leveraged Loan Transaction

As in all loans, the credit evaluation of the borrower involves a thorough understanding of the purpose and terms of the credit, the borrower's capacity to repay, and the quality of secondary repayment sources. Proper evaluation of these fundamental elements is also critical to the proper assessment of both transactional and portfolio risk in a leveraged transaction.

Understanding the purpose of the leveraged financing is the first step in evaluating the credit. A leveraged structure often signals potential increases in expected income sources, or gains in operating efficiencies or synergies. For instance, a transaction involving the merger or acquisition of a company may contain assumptions about potential synergies from the elimination of duplicate fixed costs, tax benefits, gains in managerial and human resource skills, and enhanced revenue opportunities. Alternatively, dividend recapitalizations or stock buyouts are transactions aimed primarily at increasing investor return or guarding against outside acquisitions, and substitute debt for equity. They generally do not signal enhanced revenue or operating efficiency opportunities.

Credit structure and repayment terms are often influenced by projected earnings performance, investor and market demand, and secondary support coverage. In other words, the timing of expected cash flows, investor repayment preferences, and the existence and life of collateral support will affect repayment terms. Competitive factors arising from robust market liquidity generally create more liberal repayment structures, while tightened market liquidity may allow banks to obtain more conservative covenant and repayment requirements from borrowers.

Regardless of these market shifts, it is important to understand the borrower's complete debt structure and contractual demands, priority levels, and repayment capacity in all market conditions. Bankers and examiners need to incorporate the entire leveraged lending structure into their loan quality analysis and to evaluate cash flows, working assets, and other collateral against all the debt they support. They should analyze collateral values, advance rates, and cross-collateral and cross-default agreements within the context of repayment sources, schedules, and priorities, under both normal and stressed conditions.

The assessment of the borrower's capacity to repay requires a thorough review of past operating performance and an understanding of the key drivers to achieve future operating projections. Cash flow sources must be weighed against cash needs on a recurring basis. Revenue and expense projections should avoid overly optimistic or unsubstantiated assumptions. The borrower's ongoing cash needs should include provisions for all recurring charges commensurate with the business model. This includes expenditures for the maintenance of fixed assets, tax liabilities, dividend payout expectations, and realistic repayment programs.

Examiners should expect leveraged loans to have reasonable terms and be repaid within reasonable time frames. Examiners should also carefully review uses of cash by the borrower to ensure that funds anticipated to amortize debt are not used for discretionary purposes (dividends, distributions, repayment of subordinate debt, capital expenditures, etc.) at the expense of debt repayment.

Examiners should analyze the extent to which primary and secondary sources of repayment are related in order to assess both the risk of default and the risk of loss in the event of default. Special attention should be paid to loans where repayment relies on projected cash flows, profits, or asset values that exceed historical levels. Both historical and projected factors must be considered in the evaluation of expected borrower performance. These performance, repayment, and collateral value projections should be thoroughly evaluated for reasonableness and stress tested, both at loan inception and on an ongoing basis. This includes comparing actual performance with projections and identifying the reasons for significant variances.

Understanding Enterprise Value

Methods of Assessing Enterprise Value

Conventional appraisal theory provides three approaches for valuing closely held businesses – asset, income, and market. Asset approach methods look to an enterprise's underlying assets in terms of its net going-concern or liquidation value. Income approach methods look at an enterprise's ongoing cash flows or earnings and apply appropriate capitalization or discounting techniques. Market approach methods derive value multiples from comparable company data or sales transactions. Although value estimates should reconcile results from the use of all three approaches, the most common and reliable method is the income approach.

Generally, two methods comprise the income approach. The *"capitalized cash flow"* method determines the value of a company as the present value of all the future cash flows that the business can generate in perpetuity. An appropriate cash flow is determined and then divided by a risk-adjusted capitalization rate, most commonly the weighted average cost of capital. This method is most appropriate when cash flows are predictable and stable. The *"discounted cash flow"* method is a multiple-period valuation model that converts a future series of cash flows into current value by discounting those cash flows at a rate of return (discount rate) that reflects the risk inherent therein and matches the cash flow. This method is most appropriate when future cash flows are cyclical or variable between periods. All methods are supported by numerous assumptions. Supporting documentation should therefore fully explain the appraiser's reasoning and conclusions.

Whatever the methodology, the assumptions underlying enterprise valuations should be clearly documented, well supported, and understood by appropriate decision-makers and risk oversight units. Examiners should ensure that the valuation approach is appropriate for the company's industry and condition.

Relying on Enterprise Value in Adverse Conditions

Lenders often rely upon enterprise value and other intangible values when underwriting leveraged loans to evaluate the feasibility of a loan request, to determine the debt reduction potential of planned asset sales, to assess a borrower's ability to access the capital markets, and to provide a secondary source of repayment. Also, during the life of the facility, lenders view enterprise value as a useful benchmark for assessing the sponsor's economic incentive to provide outside capital support.

When conditions for the borrower are adverse, determining whether to use enterprise value as a potential source of repayment is more complicated because the assumptions used for key variables such as cash flow, earnings, and sale multiples must reflect the adverse conditions. These variables can have a high degree of uncertainty — sales and cash flow projections may not be achieved; comparable sales may not be available; and changes can occur in a firm's competitive position, industry outlook, or the economic environment.

Because of these uncertainties, changes in the value of a firm's assets must be tested under a range of stress scenarios, including business conditions more adverse than the base case scenario. Stress testing of enterprise values and their underlying assumptions should be conducted both at origination of the loan and periodically thereafter, incorporating the actual performance of the borrower and any adjustments to projections. The bank should in all cases perform its own discounted cash flow analysis to validate the enterprise value implied by proxy measures such as multiples of cash flow, earnings, or sales.

Because enterprise value is commonly derived from the cash flows of a business, it is closely correlated with the primary source of repayment. This interdependent relationship between primary and secondary repayment sources increases the risk in leveraged financing, especially when credit weaknesses develop. Events or changes in business conditions that negatively affect a company's cash flow will also negatively affect the value of the business, simultaneously eroding both the lender's primary and secondary sources of repayment. Consequently, lenders that place undue reliance upon enterprise value as a secondary source of repayment, or that use unrealistic assumptions to determine enterprise value, are likely to approve unsound loans at origination or experience higher losses upon default.

Valuations derived with even the most rigorous valuation procedures are imprecise and may not be realized when needed by an institution. Therefore, institutions relying on enterprise value, or other illiquid and hard-to-value collateral, must have lending policies that provide for appropriate loan-to-value ratios, discount rates, and collateral margins.

Risk-Rating Guidelines for Troubled Leveraged Loans

Cash Flow/Debt Service Coverage

Examiners should pay particular attention to the adequacy of the borrower's cash flow and the reasonableness of projections. Before entering into a leveraged financing transaction, bankers should conduct an independent, realistic assessment of the borrower's ability to achieve the projected cash flow under varying economic and interest rate scenarios. This assessment should take into account the potential effects of an economic downturn or other adverse business conditions on the borrower's cash flow and collateral values. When evaluating individual borrowers, examiners should pay particular attention to:

- The overall performance and profitability of a borrower and its industry over time, including periods of economic or financial adversity.
- The history and stability of a borrower's market share, earnings, and cash flow, particularly over the most recent business cycle and last economic downturn.
- The relationship between a borrower's projected cash flow and debt service requirements and the resulting margin of debt service coverage.
- The level and composition of the borrower's recurring cash needs and fixed charges, including the nature and extent of capital expenditures, cash taxes, and dividend payments.

Examiners should adversely risk-rate a credit if material questions exist as to the borrower's ability to achieve the projected necessary cash flows, or if orderly repayment of the debt is in doubt. Credits supported by only minimal cash flow available for debt service are usually subject to an adverse rating when the credit analysis indicates that cash flows are not likely to materially increase in the near future, and hence refinancing is the only viable repayment option.

When assessing debt service capacity, examiners should use realistic repayment terms when overly liberal repayment terms or extended principal repayment requirements are coincident with unsupported or unrealistic cash flow and asset value projections. Also, loans that rely on refinancing or recapitalization as a source of repayment are largely speculative in nature. Because these repayment sources depend upon prevailing market conditions, they may be beyond the control of the borrower, and therefore the loans should have other reliable sources of repayment. Examiners should carefully analyze loans with repayment terms that continually rely on refinancing or fail to achieve successful recapitalizations.

When a borrower's condition or future prospects have significantly weakened and well-defined weaknesses in the borrower's repayment capacity are evident, leveraged finance loans will likely merit a substandard classification. If such weaknesses appear to be of a lasting nature and it is probable that a lender will be unable to collect all principal and interest owed, the loan should be placed on nonaccrual and will likely have a doubtful component. If such loans are within the scope of an institution's policy for individual evaluation they should be reviewed for impairment in accordance with Financial Accounting Standards Board Statement (FAS) 114, "Accounting by Creditors for Impairment of a Loan."

Using Enterprise Value

If the primary source of repayment is inadequate and a loan is considered collateral dependent, it is generally inappropriate to consider enterprise value unless the value is well supported. Well-supported enterprise values may be evidenced by a binding purchase and sale agreement with a qualified third party or through valuations that fully consider the effect of the borrower's distressed circumstances and potential changes in business and market conditions. For such borrowers, when a portion of the loan is not protected by pledged assets or a well-supported enterprise value, examiners will generally classify the unprotected portion of the loan doubtful or loss.

The Role of Deal Sponsors

Private equity firms, parent holding companies, and individuals invest in companies through leveraged transactions and act as their financial sponsor. The debt is extended in the name of the operating company, typically without any contractual guarantee of the financial sponsor. The sponsor's primary role is to enhance investor return by increasing cash flow and, ultimately, the value of the company. Sponsorship can provide tangible and intangible benefits to the levered company. This can include access to markets or managerial expertise not available from the prior ownership structure and financial support. Although sponsors do not generally guarantee company indebtedness, they can provide financial support through maintenance agreements to support deficient cash flows and through additional capital support under certain conditions. Their ability to provide maintenance to cash flow levels can be limited by the sponsoring firm's legal charter, its financial capacity, and its economic incentive to support the company.

Informal sponsor support is not a replacement for a thorough analysis of the credit on its own merits.

Conflicts Of Interest

The legal and regulatory issues raised by leveraged transactions are numerous and complex. When a banking company plays multiple roles in leveraged finance, the interests of different customers or divisions of the institution may conflict. For example, a lender may be reluctant to employ an aggressive collection strategy with a problem borrower because of the potential impact on the value of an affiliated organization's equity interest. A lender may face pressures to provide financial or other privileged client information that could benefit an affiliated equity investor. Banks should develop appropriate policies to address potential conflicts of interest. Banks should also track aggregate totals for borrowers and sponsors to which they have a lending and equity relationship. Banks should also establish limits for such relationships.

To ensure that potential conflicts are avoided and laws and regulations are adhered to, an independent compliance function should include a review of leveraged financing activity. Banks also need to establish policies, internal controls, and risk management procedures governing complex structure finance transactions, as discussed in *OCC Bulletin 2004-22*. The bulletin incorporates the types of internal controls and risk management procedures that can assist financial institutions in identifying and addressing the reputation, legal and other risks associated with complex structured transactions. Among other things, it provides that financial institutions should have effective policies and procedures in place to identify those complex structured finance transactions that may involve heightened reputation and legal risk, to ensure that these transactions receive enhanced scrutiny by the institution, and to ensure that the institution does not participate in illegal or inappropriate transactions. It also emphasizes the critical role of an institution's board of directors and senior management in establishing a corporate-wide culture that fosters integrity, compliance with the law, and overall good business ethics.

Expanded Procedures

Objective: Determine the scope of the examination for leveraged lending.

> **Note: These procedures, while developed to address leveraged lending activities in large banks, can be modified for use in community and mid-size banks that engage in leveraged lending. These procedures should be used, as applicable, in conjunction with the "Large Bank Supervision," "Loan Portfolio Management," and "Rating Credit Risk" booklets of the *Comptroller's Handbook*. It is important for the examiner conducting the examination of leveraged lending activities to work closely with the Loan Portfolio Management (LPM) examiner or Large Bank Credit Team Leader to identify supervisory areas of concern, more closely define the extent of examination procedures to be deployed, and maximize examination efficiencies.**

1.   Review and discuss with the examiner-in-charge (EIC) the examination scope memorandum. Align the leveraged lending examination objectives with the goals of the examination or supervisory strategy. Assess resources needed for the leveraged lending review in relation to your initial analysis of portfolio risk.

2.   Review the following information in deciding whether previously identified issues require follow-up. In consultation with the EIC and LPM examiner, determine whether bank management has effectively responded to any adverse findings and carried out any commitments.

   - Previous report of examination (ROE).
   - Bank management's response to previous examination findings.
   - Previous leveraged lending examination working papers or risk assessment summary.
   - Bank correspondence concerning leveraged lending.
   - Audit reports, internal loan review reports, and working papers, if necessary.

- Supervisory strategy, overall summary, and other relevant comments in the OCC's electronic information database.

3. Obtain from the EIC the results of the Uniform Bank Performance Reports (UBPR), Bank Expert (BERT), and other OCC reports. Identify any concerns, trends, or changes in commercial lending patterns since the last examination. Examiners should be alert to growth rates, changes in portfolio composition, loan yields, maturities, and other factors that may affect credit risk.

4. Obtain the following governing documents:

    - The bank's leveraged lending and loan syndication policies.
    - Any separate underwriting guidelines for the bank's leveraged lending program.
    - Defined risk tolerance positions and risk management guidelines.
    - Policies defining objectives, controls, and limits on affiliates' investments in leveraged transactions.

5. Obtain from the examiner assigned loan portfolio management and review the following leveraged lending schedules and reports as applicable to this area:

    - Loan trial balance, past-due accounts, and nonaccruals for leveraged lending.
    - Risk-rating stratification reports, risk-rating migration reports.
    - Concentration reports and bank definitions of concentrations monitored.
    - Exception reports.
    - Problem loan status report for adversely rated leveraged loans.
    - List of "watch" credits.
    - Any management reports used to monitor the leveraged lending portfolio.
    - Any useful information obtained from the review of the minutes of the loan and discount (or similar) committee.
    - Reports related to leveraged lending that have been furnished to the loan and discount (or similar) committee or the board of directors.

- Loans on which interest is not being collected in accordance with the terms of the loan.
- Loans for which terms have been modified by a reduction of interest rate or principal payment, by a deferral of interest or principal, or by other restructuring of repayment terms.
- Loans on which interest has been capitalized after the initial underwriting.
- Participations purchased and sold since the previous examination.
- Shared National Credits.
- Organization chart of the department.
- Resumes for leveraged lending management and senior staff.
- Each officer's current lending authority.
- Any leveraged lending profitability, capital usage, and budget reports.
- Listing of deal sponsors that support leveraged loans within the bank.
- Listing of distribution fails regarding syndicated, leveraged loans originated by the bank.
- Listing of committed pipeline exposure on leveraged loans underwritten by the bank.

6. Based on analysis of the information and discussions with management, determine whether there have been any material changes in the types of customer (based on product line), underwriting criteria, volume of lending, or market focus. Your analysis should consider

- Growth and acquisitions.
- Management changes.
- Policy and underwriting changes.
- Changes in risk tolerance limits.
- Changes in external factors such as
    - National, regional, and local economy.
    - Industry outlook.
    - Regulatory framework.
    - Technological changes.

Discussions with management should cover
- How management supervises the portfolio.
- Any significant changes in policies, procedures, personnel, and control systems.
- New marketing strategies and initiatives.
- Any internal or external factors that could affect the portfolio.
- Management's perception of the leveraged lending credit culture.
- The findings of your review of internal bank reports on leveraged lending.
- The extent of syndicated distribution and participation activities, both as a buyer and seller.

7.   Based on performance of the previous steps, combined with discussions with EIC and other appropriate supervisors, determine the examination scope and how much testing is necessary.

8.   As the examination procedures are performed, test for compliance with all applicable laws, rules, and regulations, and with established policies and processes. Confirm the existence of appropriate internal controls. Identify any area that has inadequate supervision or poses undue risk. Discuss with the EIC the need to perform additional procedures.

Select from among the following procedures those necessary to meet the examination objectives. Examiners should tailor the procedures to the bank's specific activities and risks. It is seldom that all steps are required in an examination.

Quantity of Risk

Conclusion: The quantity of risk is (low, moderate, high).

Objective 1: Assess the types and levels of risk associated with individual leveraged loans and determine the appropriate classification.

1.   Select a sample of loans to be reviewed. The sample should be adequate to assess compliance with policies, procedures, applicable bank and regulatory guidance documents, and regulations; verify the accuracy of internal risk ratings; and determine the quantity of credit risk. The sample should also be used to test changes in underwriting, including borrowing base changes, and loans with over-advances. Refer to the "Sampling Methodology" booklet of the *Comptroller's Handbook* for guidance on sampling techniques.

2.   Prepare line sheets for sampled credits. Line sheets should contain sufficient information to determine the credit rating and support any criticisms of underwriting, servicing, or credit administration practices.

3.   Obtain credit files for all borrowers in the sample and document line sheets with sufficient information regarding quality, risk rating, or both. Assess how the credit risk posed by the financial condition of the borrower will affect individual loans and the portfolio. In your analysis

   • Determine the disposition of loans classified or rated special mention during the previous examination.
   • Complete a thorough financial analysis of the borrower. Keep in mind that the primary focus with leveraged lending borrowers should be on analyzing recurring capacity of cash flow to provide repayment capacity.
   • Determine whether the borrower complies with the loan agreement, including financial covenants and borrowing base requirements.
   • Evaluate the effect of external factors, such as economic conditions and the industry life cycle, upon the borrower's ability to repay.
   • Determine, for any seasonal operating advances or lines of credit, whether the trade cycle supports clean-up (complete payout) of that

portion of the debt structure by the end of the normal business cycle.

- Review any term loans and revolving lines of credit used to support permanent working capital to determine whether cash flow provides sufficient capacity for debt service. Consider
  - A realistic repayment program when contractual debt service is back loaded and not coincident with expected increases in cash flow or asset value.
  - Working capital changes and needs.
  - Discretionary and nondiscretionary capital expenditures, product development expenses, and payments to shareholders.
  - The level of other fixed payments and maintenance expenses.
  - Reasonableness of operating projections based upon past performances and strategic initiatives of the borrower.
- Assess the borrower's access to capital markets or other sources of funds for potential support.
- Evaluate the loan agreement to determine
  - Whether the loan structure is consistent with the borrower's needs.
  - What collateral secures the loans and the accuracy of collateral descriptions, documentation and lien positions.
  - Advance rates against collateral and LTV constraints.
  - Level and reasonableness of financial covenants and triggers.
- Determine compliance with the above requirements of the loan agreement. If the borrower is not in compliance, determine the root cause, and assess the impact on credit quality.

4. For the loans in the sample, assess the quality of the collateral support by

- Reviewing quality and quantity of tangible support provided.
- Reviewing independence and integrity of collateral valuation and methodology.
- Determining reliance on "enterprise value."

5. Review the frequency, quality, and independence of the bank's estimate of the company's "enterprise valuation." Consider

- Competency and independence of individuals performing evaluations.
- Methodologies utilized.
- Reasonableness of assumptions supporting projections.
- Transparency of supporting documentation.

6. Analyze any secondary support provided by guarantors, financial sponsors, and endorsers. If the underlying financial condition of the borrower warrants concern, determine the guarantor's, sponsor's, or endorser's capacity and willingness to repay the credit.

7. Assess credit risk posed by the obligor's management team (specifically, by weaknesses in the team's quality, integrity, or ability to manage current operations and future growth) by determining whether

   - The bank's internal analysis adequately addresses the ongoing quality, integrity, and depth of the borrower's management.

   - The bank has mitigated some of this risk by requiring key executives of the borrower to obtain sufficient life insurance policies payable directly to the bank, has loan covenants in place allowing the bank to reassess the borrowing relationship in the event of the loss of a key executive, or both.

8. Identify, document, and compile any policy, underwriting, and pricing exceptions in the loans sampled. If exceptions are not being accurately identified and reported, determine the cause and discuss with management. If warranted, commentary or schedules can be included in the report of examination.

9. Using a list of nonaccruing loans, test loan accrual records to determine that interest income is not being recorded.

10. Assign risk ratings to sampled credits. See "Classification Guidelines of Troubled Leveraged Loans" in this booklet's introduction for guidance.

Objective 2: Evaluate the effect of changes in underwriting standards, practices, and policies on the quantity of credit risk in the leveraged lending portfolio.

1. Review any changes to the leveraged lending policy and syndication procedures. Determine the effect on the quantity of risk.

2. Review the current underwriting guidelines or practices, and results of policy exceptions data gathered in Objective 1, Question 8. Assess how changes since the previous examination may affect the quantity of risk. This should be done in conjunction with the sample of leveraged loans reviewed. Consider changes to
    *   Advance rates.
    *   Collateral eligibility.
    *   Level of enterprise value reliance.
    *   The number and types of covenants.
    *   Repayment terms and maturities.
    *   Financial reporting requirements.

3. Determine whether changes in processes have affected the level of risk in the portfolio. For example, if the frequency, independence, or methodology of performing enterprise valuations has been changed, determine how the change will affect credit risk.

4. Analyze the level, composition, and trend of leveraged underwriting exceptions. If this information is not available from the bank's MIS, develop it using the sample of loans taken during the examination. Determine whether the underwriting exceptions are increasing the level of risk within the portfolio or whether the exceptions are being properly mitigated.

5. If quantitative factors, such as delinquency, nonaccrual, adversely rated, average or weighted average risk ratings have increased, try to determine any correlation with changes in underwriting policy or practice.

6.	Evaluate how the leveraged lending strategic plan may affect credit risk, including the risk associated with rapid growth, geographic expansion, new or increased focus on borrowers in industries to which the unit had limited or no prior exposure, new financial sponsors, etc.

Objective 3: Determine how the composition of the leveraged lending portfolio affects the quantity of risk.

1.	Review the business or strategic plan for leveraged lending. Evaluate how implementation of the plan will affect the quantity of credit risk. Consider
  - Growth goals and potential sources of new loans.
  - Growth outside the current market area.
  - New financial sponsors and industries.
  - Concentrations of credit.
  - Management's expertise, history, and experience with the plan's products and target markets.
  - Volume and nature of syndication.

2.	Analyze the composition of, and changes to, the leveraged lending portfolio, including off-balance-sheet exposure, since the previous examination. Determine the implications for the quantity of risk of the following:
  - Any significant growth.
  - Material changes in the portfolio to include
    - Changes and trends in watch, problem, special mention, classified, past due, nonaccrual, and nonperforming assets; charge-off volumes; and risk rating distribution.
    - Loans with over-advances.
    - Any significant concentrations, including geographic, industry, and sponsor concentrations.

3.	Review the portfolio to determine whether there has been any shift in the sponsor or customer base that could increase risk. Such shifts might be to sponsors or industries with which the bank has limited experience or that possess more volatile earnings streams.

---

4. Analyze portfolio risk assessments of leveraged lending that management prepared. Determine whether management's risk assessments are supported by the examiners' analysis of the loan sample.

5. Review the local, regional, and national economic trends, and assess their impact on leveraged lending portfolio risk levels. Consider whether management has reasonably factored this data into projections of loan growth and quality.

6. Compare leveraged lending portfolio performance with planned performance and ascertain the risk implications.

7. If the bank employs concentration management tools (e.g., portfolio limits, loan sales, derivatives) to control credit exposures, analyze the impact on the quantity of risk. Consider
    • The objectives of these programs.
    • Management's experience and expertise with these tools.

8. Review recent loan reviews of leveraged lending and any related audit reports. If there are any adverse trends in quantitative measures of risk or control weaknesses reported, comment on whether and how much they may increase credit risk.

9. Analyze the level, composition, and trend of documentation exceptions and determine the potential risk implications.

10. Determine the extent of direct and indirect equity investments by bank affiliates; assess the nature and level of potential conflicts of interest.

11. Analyze the extent of syndication activities regarding leveraged loans underwritten by the bank. Assess the age, nature, and level of pipeline exposure.

12. From your portfolio and transactional reviews, discussions with bank management, policy statements or other sources, ascertain

transactions that contain characteristics of complex structure finance transactions that require further review. Consider:

- Transactions with questionable economic substance or business purpose or designed primarily to exploit accounting, regulatory or tax guidelines, particularly when executed at year end or at the end of a reporting period.
- Transactions that require an equity capital commitment from the financial institution.
- Transactions with terms inconsistent with market norms (e.g., deep "in the money" options, nonstandard settlement dates, non-standard forward-rate rolls).
- Transactions using non-standard legal agreements (e.g., customer insists on using its own documents that deviate from market norms).
- Transactions involving multiple obligors or otherwise lacking transparency (e.g., use of special purpose vehicles (SPVs) or limited partnerships).
- Transactions with unusual profits or losses or transactions that give rise to compensation that appears disproportionate to the services provided or to the risk assumed by the institution.
- Transactions that raise concerns about how the client will report or disclose the transaction (e.g., derivatives with a funding component, restructuring trades with mark to market losses).
- Transactions with unusually short time horizons or potentially circular transfers of risk (either between the financial institution and customer or between the customer and other related parties).
- Transactions with oral or undocumented agreements, which, if documented, could have material legal, reputation, financial accounting, financial disclosure, or tax implications.
- Transactions that cross multiple geographic or regulatory jurisdictions, making processing and oversight difficult.
- Transactions that cannot be processed via established operations systems.
- Transactions with significant leverage.

13. In conjunction with the review of the adequacy of bank's allowance for loan and lease losses account, determine the appropriateness of methodology relative to the level of risk assessed for the leveraged

lending portfolio. Provide synopsis of results to the examiner reviewing the bank's ALLL.

14. Evaluate the level of compliance with the guidance listed on the "References" page of this booklet. Relate the level of compliance to the quantity of credit risk. Test for compliance as necessary.

15. If violations or instances of noncompliance are noted, determine whether management has taken adequate and timely corrective action.

Quality of Risk Management

Conclusion: The quality of risk management is (weak, acceptable, or strong).

Policy

Objective: Determine whether the board of directors, consistent with its duties and responsibilities, has established leveraged lending policies appropriate for the complexity and scope of the bank's operations and whether written underwriting guidance addresses important issues not included in board policies:

1. Evaluate the adequacy of the leveraged lending policy and underwriting guidance. Policy or underwriting guidance should address the following matters:
   - A definition of leveraged lending.
   - Portfolio risk exposure limits.
   - Risk exposure sublimits defining exposure by sponsor group, risk rating, and the levels of underwriting exposure and policy exceptions.
   - Approval requirements that require sufficient senior level oversight.
   - Pricing policies that ensure a prudent tradeoff between risk and return.
   - A requirement for action plans whenever cash flow, asset sale proceeds, or collateral values decline significantly from projections. Action plans should include remedial initiatives and triggers for rating downgrades, changes to accrual status, and loss recognition.
   - Appropriate loan structures.
   - Amortization requirements of term loans.
   - Collateral requirements including acceptable types of collateral, loan-to-value limits, collateral margins, and proper valuation methodologies.
   - Covenant requirements, particularly minimum interest and fixed charge coverage and maximum leverage ratios.
   - A description of how enterprise values and other intangible business values may be used.

- Minimum documentation requirements for appraisals and valuations, including enterprise values and other intangibles.
- The types of customers, financial sponsors, and industries that are acceptable.
- Acceptable types of financial statements and minimum standards for requiring, receiving, and analyzing financial data.
- Procedures for approving exceptions to policy and underwriting guidance and maintaining MIS to track those exceptions.
- Procedures and safeguards to address potential conflicts of interest. Institutions should identify and track totals for borrowers and sponsors to whom it has both a lending and equity relationship, and set appropriate limits for such relationships.

If the bank's activities include syndication and loan participation activities, additional policy guidance should address these issues:

Syndications
- Procedures for defining, managing, and accounting for distribution fails.
- Identification of any sales made with recourse and procedures for fully reflecting the risk of any such sales.
- A process to ensure that purchasers and syndicate members are provided with timely, current financial information.
- A process to determine the portion of a transaction to be held in the portfolio, and the portion and acceptable timeframe to be held-for-sale.
- Limits on aggregate volume of bridge financing.
- Procedures and MIS to identify, control, and monitor syndication pipeline exposure.
- Limits on the length of time transactions can be held in the held-for-sale account and policies for handling items that exceed those limits.
- Prompt recognition of losses in market value for loans classified as held-for-sale.
- Procedural safeguards to prevent conflicts of interest for the bank and affiliated entities, including securities firms.

Loan Participations Purchased
- Obtaining and independently analyzing full credit information before the participation is purchased and on a timely basis thereafter.
- Obtaining from the lead lender copies of all executed and proposed loan documents, legal opinions, title insurance policies, UCC searches, and other relevant documents.
- Carefully monitoring the borrower's performance throughout the life of the loan.
- Establishing appropriate risk management guidelines.

2. Determine whether the policy establishes concentration guidelines for leveraged lending and outlines actions to be taken when limits are exceeded.

3. Determine that annual reviews of leveraged lending policies and underwriting guidance are conducted by the board or an appropriate credit committee.

Processes

Objective: Determine whether lending practices, procedures, and internal controls regarding leveraged loans are adequate.

1. Evaluate how policies, procedures, and plans affecting the leveraged lending portfolio are communicated. Consider
    - Whether management has clearly communicated objectives and risk limits for the leveraged lending portfolio to the board of directors and whether the board has approved these policies.
    - Whether communication to key personnel in the leveraged lending department or to those loan officers involved in leveraged lending transactions is timely.

2. Determine whether management information systems provide timely, useful information to evaluate risk levels and trends in the leveraged lending portfolio.

3.   Assess the process to ensure the accuracy and integrity of leveraged lending data.

4.   Determine the effectiveness of processes to monitor compliance with leveraged lending policy. Consider
     - Approval and monitoring of policy limit exceptions.
     - The volume and type of exceptions including any identified in the loan sample.
     - Internal loan review, audit, and compliance process findings.

5.   Assess the underwriting process for leveraged loans. Consider the appropriateness of the approval process and the adequacy of credit analysis.

6.   Evaluate the accuracy and integrity of the internal risk rating processes. Consider
     - Findings from the loan sample.
     - The role of loan review.

7.   Assess the process to ensure compliance with applicable laws, rulings, regulations, and accounting guidelines.

8.   Evaluate the effectiveness of processes used to monitor enterprise valuations. Consider the quality, frequency, and independence of the process.

9.   The examiner reviewing the leveraged loan portfolio should review the LPM examiner's findings to determine whether additional analysis is required for issues pertaining to
     - Problem credit administration.
     - Collections.
     - Charge-offs.

10. In conjunction with the review of the Allowance for Loan and Lease Losses account, review the method of evaluating, documenting, and maintaining the account. Determine whether the method is consistent with current accounting and regulatory guidance.

11. Verify the integrity of loan documentation. Assess the quality controls ensuring that credit documentation is complete.

12. Assess the risk limits management has established, evaluating both portfolio-wide limits and less comprehensive ones. After determining how much earnings or capital is at risk, decide whether these limits are appropriate. Evaluate the plans management has developed to respond to breaches in defined risk tolerance levels.

13. Determine whether there are processes to monitor strategic and business plans for the portfolio. Consider the impact on earnings and capital as leveraged lending plans and strategies are executed.

14. Evaluate the adequacy of internal controls within the leveraged lending unit or function and the bank's process to periodically evaluate its internal review procedures.

15. Assess the bank's process to identify and safeguard against conflicts of interest.

Personnel

Objective: To determine whether management and affected personnel display acceptable knowledge and technical skills to manage and perform their duties related to leveraged lending (including specific industry knowledge when applicable).

1. Determine whether the level of expertise and number of assigned personnel in the designated leveraged lending area or function is adequate. Consider
   • Whether staffing levels will support current operations or any planned growth.
   • Staff turnover.
   • The staff's previous leveraged lending and workout experience.
   • Specialized training provided.

- The average account load per lending officer. Consider whether the load is reasonable in light of the complexity and condition of each officer's portfolio.
- How senior management and the board of directors periodically evaluate the leveraged lending unit's understanding of and conformance with the bank's stated credit culture and loan policy. If there is no evaluation, determine the impact on the management of credit risk.

2. Assess the performance management and compensation programs for leveraged lending personnel. Consider whether these programs measure and reward behaviors that support the portfolio's strategic objectives and risk tolerance limits.

Controls

Objective: To determine the adequacy of loan review, internal/external audit, management information systems, internal controls, and any other control systems for leveraged lending.

1. Assess the effectiveness and independence of formal control functions.

2. Control functions should have clear reporting lines, adequate resources, and the authority necessary to initiate change. Evaluate reporting lines to determine whether lenders could bring to bear undue influence on operations or control staff.

3. Determine the effectiveness of the loan review system in identifying risk in leveraged lending. Consider the following:
- Scope of loan review.
- Frequency of loan reviews.
- The number and qualifications of loan review personnel.
- Results of examination.
- Loan review's access to information and the board.
- Training opportunities or programs offered to loan review staff.
- Content of loan review reports, which should address

- The overall asset quality of the portfolio.
- Trends in asset quality.
- The quality of "significant" relationships.
- The level and trend of policy, underwriting, and pricing exceptions.

4. Review the most recent loan review report for the leveraged lending area. Determine whether management has appropriately addressed weaknesses and areas of unwarranted risk.

5. Assess loan review's ability to identify emerging problems.

6. Determine whether problems have to be pronounced before loan review brings them to senior management's attention.

7. Determine whether management information systems provide timely, useful information to evaluate risk levels and trends in the leveraged lending portfolio.

8. Determine the adequacy of internal audit functions for leveraged lending. Consider:
   - The scope of internal audit and results of the previous audit.
   - Frequency of audits.
   - The number and qualifications of internal audit personnel.
   - Audit's access to information and the board.
   - Adequacy and timeliness of follow-up reviews.

9. Obtain from the examiner assigned internal and external audits a list of deficiencies noted in internal and external auditors' latest reviews. Determine whether management has appropriately addressed these deficiencies.

10. Determine whether management's response to any material findings by any control group (including audit and loan review) has been verified and reviewed for objectivity and adequacy by senior management and the board (or a committee thereof).

Conclusions

Objective: Determine overall conclusions and communicate findings regarding the quantity of risk and management's ability to identify, measure, monitor, and control risk in leveraged lending. To obtain commitments from management to initiate appropriate corrective action, if necessary.

1. Prepare a summary memorandum to the LPM examiner or EIC regarding the leveraged lending portfolio. Draft conclusions on
   - Asset quality of the portfolio.
   - The adequacy of policies and underwriting standards.
   - Volume and severity of underwriting and policy exceptions.
   - Underwriting quality of sample loans.
   - Quality of portfolio supervision.
   - Concentrations of credit.
   - Adequacy and timeliness of MIS.
   - Adequacy of loan control functions.
   - Compliance with applicable laws, rules, and regulations.
   - Quality of staffing.
   - Reliability of internal risk ratings.
   - Appropriateness of strategic and business plans.
   - The extent to which leveraged lending credit risk and credit risk management practices affect aggregate loan portfolio risk.
   - Recommended corrective action regarding deficient policies, procedures, and practices. (Include whether management commits to the corrective action.)
   - Any other concerns.

2. Provide input to help the EIC assign the bank CAMELS component ratings for asset quality and management.

3. Recommend risk assessments for the leveraged lending portfolio. Refer to the "Large Bank Supervision" and "Community Bank Supervision" booklets in the *Comptroller's Handbook* for guidance.

4. Based on discussions with the EIC and bank management, and information in the summary memorandum, prepare a brief comment on leveraged lending for inclusion in the ROE.

5. Discuss examination findings and conclusions with the examiner assigned loan portfolio management and the EIC. If necessary, compose "Matters Requiring Attention" (MRA) for the loan portfolio management examination. MRAs should cover practices that

    - Deviate from sound, fundamental principles and are likely to result in financial deterioration if not addressed.
    - Result in substantive noncompliance with laws.

    MRAs should discuss

    - Causes of the problem.
    - Consequences of inaction.
    - Management's commitment to corrective action.
    - The time frame and persons responsible for corrective action.

6. Discuss findings with bank management, including conclusions about risks and risk management. Obtain commitments for corrective action.

7. Write a memorandum or update the supervisory strategy, or both, specifically setting out what the OCC should do in the future to effectively supervise the leveraged lending function at the bank. Include time frames, staffing, and workdays required.

8. Update the supervisory record and any applicable report of examination schedules or tables.

9. Update the examination work papers in accordance with OCC guidance.

Adverse Risk Rating Examples

Example A of Adverse Risk Ratings

Borrower: United Publication Company, Inc. (United)
Yourtown, USA

Business: Publisher of several monthly brand-name specialty magazines and provider of media production services.

Facility (Facilities) Description:

1. $50 million RC with maturity in one year. $20 million outstanding.
2. $50 million TL-A with current balance $45 million originating one year ago. Maturity in five years. Interest quarterly.
3. $200 million TL-B. Maturity in six years. Interest quarterly.
4. $400 million TL-C. Maturity in six years. Interest quarterly.

Credit agreement covering facilities has been amended three times, reducing annual principal repayment and financial covenant requirements. Total senior secured financing of $700 million shares its position in right of payment with additional high yield debt of $750 million.

Pricing: LIBOR + 200 BP.

Repayment: TL-A amortizes $5 million annually with $30MM balance due at maturity.
TL-B amortizes $2 million annually with $190 million balance due at maturity.
TL-C is due at maturity.

Purpose: Debt refinancing and portfolio acquisitions.

Primary Repayment Source:

Operating cash flow.

Secondary Repayment Source:

Sale of individual operating units, publications, and trademarks.

Covenant Compliance:

Yes, as amended.

Collateral: All business assets. No collateral valuation.

Financial Synopsis:

- Financial condition is characterized by high leverage and negative tangible net worth. Working capital position is deficit and liquidity is provided by RC. Senior and total debt represent 6.5X and 7.5X EBITDA, respectively.
- Principal assets are goodwill $1 billion and intangible assets $250 million.
- Recent asset sales were used to prepay high yield debt resulting in the current balance above, but do support value of branded publications.
- Earnings and performance levels are stable, but company has not realized growth plans that were basis for underwriting.
- Current FYE fixed charge coverage (FCC) is projected to be 1.0X and benefits from the deferred amortization schedule of senior debt.

Current Status: United's current cash flow projections reflect capacity to meet contractual debt service requirements with little additional margin. Management will continue efforts to divest marginal units to reduce debt levels.

Risk Rating Decision:

Substandard/Accrual

- Weak financial position, characterized by high leverage, deficit working capital and negative tangible net worth.
- Operating performance below projected levels.
- Senior debt repayment restructure is liberal. Available operating cash flow provides for payment of interest, but only nominal reduction in company's high debt level.
- Sales of several underperforming units and the current performance levels of remaining units support the estimated value of remaining brand name units and exceed total senior debt.
- Accrual status is supported by the stability and capacity of operating cash flow to provide interest payments.

Risk Rating Considerations:

- Ability of the company to meet contractual debt service requirements does not mitigate its inability to provide reasonable level of debt reduction from operating cash flow.
- Company management has been unable to increase revenues as planned and has resorted to secondary repayment sources (asset divestitures) to reduce debt.
- Stability of earnings streams from remaining name brand units supports their estimated value.
- Capacity of operating earnings to meet interest charges supports continued accrual status.

Example B of Adverse Risk Ratings

Borrower: Consolidated Equipment Company, Inc. (Consolidated) Anytown, USA

Business: Manufacturer of transportation equipment.

Facility Description:

$200 million RC with maturity due in three years. RC fully drawn. Outstanding balance recently permanently reduced $50 million by sale of three divisions.

Pricing: LIBOR + 250 BP.

Repayment: Interest due monthly, principal at maturity. Required step-down in commitment not met.

Purpose: Debt restructure and merger-related expenses.

Primary Repayment Source:

Operating cash flow.

Secondary Repayment Source:

Sale of business assets or sale and refinance of company stock, or both.

Covenant Compliance:

No. Violated six covenants at last FYE. Covenants have subsequently been waived for this year in exchange for $15 million equity injection.

Collateral: First lien on nine manufacturing plants recently independently appraised at $15 million, M&E appraised by third party using orderly liquidation value at $10 million, and AR with book value $10 million. Last field audit of company's AR's reflects significant delinquencies with no subsequent follow-up.

Enterprise Value: Estimated between $200 million and $250 million. Values have declined significantly with company's deteriorating financial condition. The valuation relies on an increase in sales volume and margin beginning next year. Success of the plan is dependent on an industry turnaround and is hindered by the company's current distressed condition.

Financial Synopsis:

- Financial condition is characterized by high leverage and minimal tangible net worth.
- Liquidity and working capital relief are only temporary in duration and provided by a recent $15 million, one-time equity infusion after the vendors refused to extend trade credit.
- Total debt structure includes $75 million in subordinated debt.
- Earnings and performance levels are poor. Expected synergies and improved sales projected from merger have not materialized. Sales levels have actually declined from pre-merger levels from a shift in customer preference and industry slowdown.
- Last two FYE results show a breakeven EBITDA level and insufficient capacity to make interest payments. Proceeds of the recent sale of three divisions were used to reduce RC facility.

Current Status: Consolidated has incurred large operating losses since the merger of the two predecessor companies. The company experienced a significant decline in equipment orders and industry outlook is unfavorable for the near future. Current cash flow projections do not reflect capacity to meet contractual debt service requirements with questionable liquidity sources.

Risk Rating Decision:

Split rating – Substandard/Doubtful. Interest on Nonaccrual

- Weak financial position, characterized by high leverage, deficit working capital and minimal tangible net worth.
- Liquidity level continues to pose an immediate threat to the company with limited sources.
- Operating performance is poor and not expected to improve significantly in near future.
- Cash flow is incapable of providing for company's liquidity needs and supporting ongoing capital needs, debt repayment, and interest costs.
- Appraised value of hard assets (RE and M&E) supported by current, independent appraisals classified substandard ($25 million). Remainder of debt collateralized by questionable value of delinquent AR and secondary support provided by enterprise value classified doubtful ($125 million). Portion of RC permanently reduced by sale of three divisions not classified ($50 million).
- Borrower's questionable ability to repay principal and interest requires the nonaccrual of interest.

Risk Rating Considerations:

- The level of secondary support provided by the company's enterprise value is suspect due to the company's severely distressed condition, immediate liquidity concerns, insufficient cash flow, and poor industry conditions.

Example C of Adverse Risk Ratings

Borrower: Many Promotional Items, Inc. (Many)
Mytown, USA

Business: Supplier of promotional products.

Facility Description:
$300 million aggregate balance recently restructured into three TL tranches all maturing in five years.
TL-A $150 million, TL-B $100 million, and TL-C $50 million.

Pricing: TL-A: LIBOR + 250.
TL-B: 8 percent PIK.
TL-C: No interest, convertible into 25 percent of common stock at lender's option.

Repayment: TL-A: Interest monthly plus $1 million quarterly principal payments. Semi-annual cash flow recapture per formula.
TL-B: PIK interest due annually. Principal due at maturity.
TL-C: No interest. Principal due at maturity.

Purpose: Restructuring of outstanding debts originally used for acquisition financing and working capital.

Primary Repayment Source:
Operating cash flow, sale of business, or refinance.

Secondary Repayment Source:
Sale of business or refinance, or both.

Covenant Compliance:

Not in compliance before recent restructuring, violating EBITDA, leverage and interest coverage covenants. All violations waived as part of restructure. Following restructure, all covenants are in compliance.

Collateral:

TL-A: All company assets and stock of subsidiaries and borrower. TL-B and TL-C: Second lien on all company assets and stock of subsidiaries and borrower. Facilities are defaulted. AR and INV are subordinated to another lender. Collateral not audited or formally monitored. Estimated value of FA $50 million. Estimated equity net of first lien in AR and INV is $50 million.

Enterprise Value:

Independently estimated between $150 million and $180 million.

Financial Synopsis:

- Financial position reflects significant deterioration over the past three years with severe leverage, negative tangible net worth, excessive operating losses and inadequate CF.
- Financial stress is a result of Many's leveraged acquisition strategy initiated two years ago and failure to effectively integrate acquired entities to achieve projected results.
- Last FYE operating statement reflects the erosion of revenues by 10 percent from the prior year, and trailing management projections by 20 percent.
- The year produced a FCC of only .43X, leverage increasing with funded debt/EBITDA at 10X, and intangibles representing 30 percent of total assets.

Current Status:

- A new management team has been put into place and has reduced operating costs but not yet demonstrated success to restore company stability.
- Current interim financial results reflect results in line with reduced expectations, but success is dependent on ability to achieve a moderate revenue turnaround and controlling overhead over a sustained fiscal time period.
- Projections for the next two years reflect a stable level of free cash flow consistent with current performance at $20 million. Projected CF ramp ups after year three are suspect due to company's lack of demonstrated ability to achieve shorter-term projections and economic uncertainties.

Risk Rating Decision:

Split rating – Substandard/Doubtful/Loss. Interest on Nonaccrual

- Weak financial position, characterized by high leverage and negative tangible worth.
- Operating losses continue to inhibit cash flow and jeopardize full and orderly liquidation of debt.
- Portion of TL-A supported by the reasonable repayment capacity of the current level of sustainable free cash flow is classified substandard ($100 million).
- Portion of TL-A supported by the more speculative nature of the EntV dependent upon significant cash flow ramp-ups after the first two years is classified doubtful ($50 million).
- TL-B and C are not supported by past or near term financial performance of the company or available secondary sources, and are classified loss ($150 million).
- Borrower's inability to repay principal and interest requires the nonaccrual of interest.

Risk Rating Considerations:

- The level of secondary support provided by the company's EntV is suspect due to the company's poor performance to date, but risk of loss is much higher on that portion supported by long-term projected improvement in cash flow.

▯everaged ▯ending — Appendix B

▯ lossary

Ac▯ uisition — When one company purchases a majority interest in the acquired. Acquisitions can be either friendly or unfriendly. Friendly acquisitions occur when the target firm agrees to be acquired; unfriendly acquisitions don't have the same agreement from the target firm.

Air▯ all — The portion of a loan whose value exceeds the value of its underlying collateralized assets, and dependent upon support provided by the company's enterprise value. Also know as the "financing gap."

Best efforts syndication — This refers to a type of loan syndication. See also **underwritten deal** and **clu▯ deal**. In a best efforts syndication, the underwriter agrees to use all efforts to sell as much of the loan as possible. If the underwriter is unable to sell the entire amount of the loan, it is not responsible for any unsold portions. However, **flex** (see also) language may be negotiated to facilitate the arranger(s) gaining market acceptance for the credit.

Bookrunner — The lead bank on a deal.

Bridge e▯ uity — A short term equity investment in a company that is expected to be replaced by future equity sales to permanent investors. Bridge equity is provided, at times, by a bank holding company or subsidiary to facilitate the underwriting process.

Bridge loan — A short term loan or security which is expected to be replaced by permanent financing (debt or equity securities, loan syndication or asset sales) prior to the maturity date of the loan. Bridge loans may include an unfunded commitment, as well as funded amounts, and generally mature in one year or less.

Buy▯ ack — The buying back of outstanding shares (repurchase) by a company in order to reduce the number of shares on the market. Companies will buyback shares either to increase the value of shares still available (reducing supply), or to eliminate any threats by shareholders who may be looking for a controlling stake. A buyback is a method for company to invest in itself since it can't own itself. Thus, buybacks reduce the number of shares outstanding on the market, which increases the proportion of shares the company owns. Buybacks can be carried out in two ways:

- Shareholders may be presented with a tender offer whereby they have the option to submit (or tender) a portion or all of their shares within a certain time frame and at a premium to the current market price. This premium compensates investors for tendering their shares rather than holding on to them.
- Companies buy back shares on the open market over an extended period.

Club deal — This is a type of loan syndication. See also **best efforts syndication** and **underwritten deal.** A club deal is usually a smaller credit, $25 million to $50 million, which an arranger markets to a small group of relationship lenders. A club deal may not be governed by a single loan agreement; however, participating lenders usually have very similar, if not identical, terms.

Covenant lite — Refers to syndicated loans that have bond-like **incurrence covenants** (see also), if any covenants, rather than traditional **maintenance covenants** (see also).

Covenant headroom — Covenant headroom compares the credit statistics from the projected financials (one year out) with the first covenant compliance levels. For example, for a transaction that provides pro forma financials as of July 31, covenant headroom analysis is based upon the projected debt/EBITDA ratio from the financial model at December 31 versus the maximum debt/EBITDA covenant level allowed on the same date. Covenant headroom analysis calculates how much performance can deteriorate before the covenant is tripped or violated.

Convertible bond — A bond that can be converted into a predetermined amount of the company's equity at certain times during its life, usually at the discretion of the bondholder. Issuing convertible bonds is one way for a company to minimize negative investor interpretation of its corporate actions. For example, if an already public company chooses to issue stock, the market usually interprets this as a sign that the company's share price is somewhat

---

overvalued. To avoid this negative impression, the company may choose to issue convertible bonds, which bondholders will likely convert to equity anyway should the company continue to do well. From the investor's perspective, a convertible bond has a value-added component built into it; it is essentially a bond with a stock option hidden inside. Thus, it tends to offer a lower rate of return in exchange for the value of the option to trade the bond into stock.

Cross default — A provision in a bond indenture or loan agreement that puts the borrower in default if the borrower defaults on another obligation. Also known as "cross acceleration." This provides more security to the lender. This provision can be considered as an "out-clause" to the contract.

Debt🗌Equity swap — A refinancing deal in which a debt holder gets an equity position in exchange for cancellation of the debt. There are several reasons why a company may want to swap debt for equity. For example, a firm may be in financial trouble and a debt/equity swap could help avoid bankruptcy, or the company may want to change capital structure to take advantage of current stock valuation. Bond indenture covenants may prevent a swap from occurring without consent.

Dividend recapitalization — When a company incurs a new debt in order to pay a special dividend to private investors or shareholders. This usually involves a company owned by a private investment firm, which can authorize a dividend recapitalization as an alternative to selling its equity stake in the company (also known as a "dividend recap.") The dividend recap has seen explosive growth, primarily as an avenue for private investment firms to recoup some or all of the money they used to purchase their stake in a business. It is generally not looked upon favorably by creditors or common shareholders because it reduces the credit quality of the company while only benefiting a select few.

EBITDA — Earnings Before Interest, Taxes, Depreciation, and Amortization. EBITDA can be used to analyze and compare profitability between companies and industries because it eliminates the effects of financing and accounting decisions. EBITDA is a good metric to evaluate profitability, but not cash flow as it leaves out the cash required to fund working capital and the replacement of old equipment.

Enterprise value — A measure of a company's value as a going concern. Three primary approaches are commonly used for valuing closely held businesses – asset, income, and market. The asset approach method looks to an enterprise's underlying assets in terms of its net going concern or liquidation value. The income approach method looks at an enterprise's ongoing cash flows or earnings and applies appropriate capitalization or discounting techniques. The market approach method derives value multiples from guideline company data or transactions.

Equity financing — The act of raising money for company activities by selling common or preferred stock to individual or institutional investors. In return for the money paid, shareholders receive ownership interests in the corporation (also known as "share capital.") This is when a company raises money by issuing stock. The other way to raise money is through debt financing, which is when the company borrows money.

Equity kickers — Also called equity sweetener, offer ownership in exchange for a loan or other debt instrument. Convertible features (stock options) and warrants are offered as equity kickers by a company to a lender or other party as an inducement to lend money to a company or provide some other value. In a leveraged buy out transaction, equity kickers give potential additional returns to mezzanine financers if the transaction is successful.

Financing gap — See Airball

Fixed Charge Coverage Ratio (FCCR) — A financial ratio used to measure earnings before income taxes, interest payments, and noncash expenses to fixed charges. Fixed charges usually include CAPEX, taxes, debt repayment, interest, and dividend payment requirements.

Flex language — Contract terms negotiated between the borrower and syndicate arranger prior to syndication. Such language may refer to price, structure or both and is put in place to help ensure the deal will clear market, e.g., successfully syndicate. Price flex allows the arranger to adjust credit pricing, usually within a specified range, to ensure successful syndication. Structure flex allows the arranger to adjust deal structure within certain pre-negotiated parameters to ensure market clearance. Structural flex provisions may allow the arranger to reallocate amounts between tranches, add or remove covenants, adjust covenant levels, etc.

Fronting/Fronted facilities — Fronting is an arrangement in which the lender advances loans or foreign currencies or issues L/Cs on behalf of a consortium. Immediately upon issuance of the advance, L/C or other instrument, the risk is prorated to the consortium. Each lender in the lender group is deemed to have purchased from the fronting bank a participation in that advance, in an amount equal to that lender's applicable commitment percentage. For L/Cs, although the agent bank issues the L/C for the full amount, immediately after issuance of the L/C the risk is prorated out to the consortium.

Headroom — See **covenant headroom.**

Highly leveraged transaction (HLT) — Term referencing the following rescinded regulatory definition of a leveraged loan. "(A)n extension of credit to or investment in a business by an insured depository institution where the financing transaction involves a buyout, acquisition, or recapitalization of an existing business and one of the following criteria is met: (1) The transaction results in a liabilities-to-assets leverage ratio higher than 75 percent; or (2) The transaction at least doubles the subject company's liabilities and results in a liabilities-to-assets leverage ratio higher than 50 percent; (3) the transaction is designated an HLT by a syndication agent or a federal bank regulator." (Rescinded Banking Circular 242, "Definition of Highly Leveraged Transactions.")

Incurrence covenants — Loan covenants that generally require if an issuer takes an action (paying a dividend, making an acquisition, issuing more debt), the resultant position would need to remain in compliance. An issuer that has an incurrence test that limits its debt to 5x cash flow would only be able to take on more debt if, on a pro forma basis, it was still within this constraint. If not, then it would have breeched the covenant and would be in default. If, on the other hand, an issuer found itself above this 5x threshold simply because its earnings had deteriorated, it would not violate the covenant.

Initial public offering (IPO) — The first sale of stock by a private company to the public. IPO's are often issued by smaller, newer companies seeking capital to expand, but can also be done by large privately-owned companies looking to become publicly traded.

In an IPO, the issuer obtains the assistance of an underwriting firm, which helps it determine what type of security to issue (common or preferred), best offering price and time to bring it to market.

Institutional loan — See also **pro rata**. Those **tranches** (see also) in a syndicated credit that are specifically structured for institutional investors (primarily collateralized loan obligations (CLOs) insurance companies, and pension funds), although there are some banks that may buy institutional credits. Traditionally, institutional loans were referred to as term loan B's (TLBs) because they were bullet payment or with nominal (1 percent per annum was common) amortization. Now institutional loans refer to tranches other than the revolver and term loan A (TLA).

Junk Bond — A bond rated "BB" or lower because of its high default risk. Also known as a "high-yield bond" or "speculative bond." These are usually purchased for speculative purposes. Junk bonds typically offer interest rates three to four percentage points higher than safer government issues.

Leveraged Buyout (LBO) — The acquisition of another company using a significant amount of borrowed money (bonds or loans) to meet the cost of acquisition. Often, the assets of the company being acquired are used as collateral for the loans in addition to the assets of the acquiring company. The purpose of leveraged buyouts is to allow companies to make large acquisitions without having to commit a lot of capital.

Leveraged loan — A term broadly applied to a type of loan where the obligor's post-financing leverage, when measured by debt to assets, debt to equity, cash flow to total debt, or other such standards unique to particular industries, significantly exceeds industry norms for leverage. The proceeds for such loans are generally used for buyouts, acquisition, or recapitalization.

Loan syndication — The process of involving multiple lenders in providing various portions of a loan. A syndicated loan is structured, arranged and administered by one or several commercial or investment banks known as arrangers. Syndication allows any one lender to provide a large loan while maintaining a more prudent and manageable credit exposure because it isn't the only creditor. The bank regulatory agencies define a shared national credit as a loan of $20 million or more syndicated among three or more regulated institutions.

Loss given default — The amount of loss recognized by a bank or other financial institution when a borrower defaults on a loan.

Material adverse change (MAC) clause — The term, also sometimes called "material adverse effect," describes an occurrence, event or condition that could or would likely cause a long-term and significant diminution in the earnings power or value of a business. The phrase is commonly used in venture investment or merger and acquisition transactions in connection with a closing condition whereby the investor/acquirer has the benefit of a "walk" right if the target company experiences a serious adverse change between the date the contract is signed and the transaction closing date.

Maintenance covenants — Loan covenants requiring an issuer to meet certain financial tests every reporting period, usually quarterly. If a borrower's loan agreement contains a maintenance covenant, which limits debt to cash flow, the borrower would violate the covenant if debt increased or earnings deteriorated sufficiently to breach the specified level.

Merger — The combining of two or more companies, generally by offering the stockholders of one company securities in the acquiring company in exchange for the surrender of their stock. This decision is usually mutual between both firms.

Mezzanine financing — A hybrid of debt and equity financing that is typically used to finance the expansion of existing companies. Mezzanine financing is debt capital that gives the lender the rights to convert to an ownership or equity interest in the company if the loan is not paid back in time and in full. It is generally subordinated to debt provided by senior lenders such as banks and venture capital companies.

Since mezzanine financing is usually provided to the borrower very quickly with little due diligence on the part of the lender and little or no collateral on the part of the borrower, this type of financing is aggressively priced with the lender seeking a return in the 20 to 30 percent range. Mezzanine financing is advantageous because it is treated like equity on a company's balance sheet and may make it easier to obtain standard bank financing. To attract mezzanine financing, a company usually must demonstrate a track record in the industry with an established reputation and product, a history of profitability and a viable expansion plan for the business (e.g. expansions, acquisitions, IPO).

Pari passu — A Latin phrase meaning "by an equal progress" or "without preference." The term's use by creditors reflects that lenders share equally in the collateral or other asset pool.

Payment in kind ⏿P⏿ ⏿ — The capitalization of interest. The use of additional debt as payment for interest instead of cash.

Private e⏿ uity — Equity capital that is made available to companies or investors, but not quoted on a stock market. The funds raised through private equity can be used to develop new products and technologies, to expand working capital, to make acquisitions, or to strengthen a company's balance sheet.

Pro⏿ a⏿ ility of default — The degree of likelihood that the borrower will not be able to make scheduled payments. Should the borrower be unable to pay, it is then said to be in default of the debt, at which point the lenders of the debt have legal avenues to attempt obtaining at least partial repayment.

Pro rata — See also **institutional loan**. A Latin phrase meaning "proportionately." For example, the creditors of the same class are to be paid pro rata; that is, each is to receive payment at the same ratio to their claim that the aggregate of assets bears to the aggregate of debts. In syndicated lending, pro rata debt usually refers to the revolving credit and the amortizing TLA.

Recapitali⏿ ation — Historically, recapitalization frequently referred to injecting some form of capital into a distressed company to improve its condition. Currently when used in relation to a leveraged loan, recapitalization (also referred to as a **dividend recap**, see also) usually means to extract funds from a company by using debt to pay a dividend. Financial sponsors are motivated to take this action to extract their investment and increase their return. Existing company management sometimes takes this step as a defensive measure. By doing a dividend recap, they return money to current shareholders by levering the company, making it unattractive as a take over candidate and consequently protecting current management.

Revolving credit ⬜RC⬜ facility — A line of credit in which the customer pays a commitment fee and is then allowed to use the funds when they are needed. It is usually used for operating purposes, fluctuating each month depending on the customer's current cash flow needs. Often referred to as a revolver or RC.

Risk of default — The risk that the borrower will be unable to pay the contractual interest or principal on their debt obligations.

Second lien loans — Second lien loans or last-out-tranche loans are typically subordinated in their rights to receive principal and interest payments from the borrower to the rights of the holders of senior debt. As a result, second lien debt is riskier than senior debt.

Senior de⬜t — A form of debt that takes priority over other debt securities sold by the issuer. In the event the issuer goes bankrupt, senior debt must be repaid before other creditors receive any payment.

Springing lien — A provision in a credit agreement that gives creditors a lien on specific collateral only if the borrower's financial condition deteriorates to or beyond a specific measure of credit quality such as an outside credit agency rating.

Swing line facility — Provides the borrower with the ability to request smaller minimum advances than that allowed under a revolving credit facility, up to a maximum amount. Upon an advance under a swing line, each lender in the bank group is deemed to have purchased from the swing line lender a participation in that advance. The swing line facility typically reduces the transfers of funds between the agent and members of the bank group to such times as participations in, or refinancing of, the swing line are requested by the borrower or swing line lender. The swing line is effectively a sublimit of a syndicated revolving credit and is typically not discretionary on the part of the lenders unless so specified in the credit agreement.

Term loan A — Loan made for a specific amount that has a specified repayment schedule. Term loans usually mature beyond one year with proceeds used for long-term capital needs.

Term loan B — Institutional term loans or term loans that are sold to institutional investors such as prime funds, CLOs, insurance companies, etc.

Toggle note — A toggle note gives the borrower the option of cash pay interest or **payment in kind** (see also). A toggle note is an **institutional tranche** (see also) and usually has nominal or no principal reduction until maturity. It is usually cash pay interest at inception and toggling (hence the name) the note to PIK usually results in a rate increase to compensate debt holders for no longer receiving cash interest.

Tranches — (French: slice) Piece, portion, or slice of a deal or structured financing. This portion is one of several related securities that are offered at the same time but have different risks, rewards or maturities. Tranche is a term often used to describe a specific class within an offering wherein each tranche offers varying degrees of risk to the investor or lender. For example, a structured offering might have tranches that have one-year, two-year, five-year and ten-year maturities. It can also refer to segments that are offered domestically and internationally.

Underwritten deal — This refers to a type of syndication. See also **best efforts syndication** and **club deal**. An underwritten deal is one in which the arranger(s) guarantee the entire commitment then syndicate the loan. If the arranger(s) cannot fully syndicate the loan, they must absorb the difference, which they may later try to sell to investors.

Accounting for Leveraged Lending

This appendix highlights key accounting requirements with respect to leveraged lending. While it highlights the pertinent accounting, it is not a substitute for the actual standards. These standards evolve over time. Bankers and examiners should ensure the standards they follow are current. Examiners should contact the Office of the Chief Accountant if accounting issues arise.

Commitment to Lend

For leveraged lending commitments to originate loans where the fair value option under Statement of Financial Accounting Standards (FAS) No. 159, "The Fair Value Option for Financial Assets and Financial Liabilities," has been elected, the commitments would be recorded at fair value with gains and losses recognized in current period earnings.

When FAS 159 is not elected, the commitments would not be recorded at fair value; however, banks may need to recognize losses related to these commitments. The determination and consideration of any such losses depends on the bank's intent to either sell or hold the loan after origination.

Loan commitments that relate to loans that a bank intends to hold for investment should be evaluated for credit impairment in accordance with FAS 5, "Accounting for Contingencies." Similar to the accounting for loans held for investment, losses on commitments for these loans should be based on credit related losses, not market related losses. Loan commitments, or portions of loan commitments, that the company intends to sell should not be considered held for investment.

For loan commitments that relate to loans a bank intends to hold for sale, there are two acceptable alternatives for accounting. Under Alternative A, the bank accounts for these loan commitments at the lower of cost or fair value. The bank should recognize any loss and record a liability to the extent that the terms of the committed loans are below current market terms.

Under Alternative B, the bank accounts for these loan commitments under FAS 5. If it is probable that the loan will be funded and then held for sale, any loss related to market conditions should be recognized and a related liability recognized (even though the commitment has not yet been funded). Both interest rate and credit risk should be considered in measuring the fair value of the commitment.

Under both Alternative A and Alternative B, the premise is that it is inappropriate to delay recognition of a loss related to declines in the fair value of a loan commitment until the date a loan is funded and classified as held for sale. If it is probable that a loss has been incurred because it is probable that an existing loan commitment will be funded and the loan will be sold at a loss, then the loss on that commitment should be recognized in earnings.

Banks should follow the guidance in FAS 157, "Fair Value Measurements," in estimating the fair value of loan commitments. Under FAS 157 "fair value" is defined as the price that would be received to sell an asset or paid to transfer a liability in an orderly transaction between market participants. In the absence of an active market, loan commitments should be valued using valuation techniques that are appropriate for the circumstances and consider what a third party would pay to acquire the commitments, or demand to assume the commitments. The method that banks use to estimate the fair value should be reasonable, well supported, and adequately documented.

OCC Advisory Letter 99-4 (AL 99-4) states, "Agent banks should clearly define their hold level before syndication efforts begin." Generally there is no prohibition in GAAP for a bank to change their intent to sell. However, to comply with AL 99-4, and as the accounting is affected by intent, adequate "intent" documentation should be completed in a timely manner. This would include the bank's rationale for the change in intent and their analysis from a credit and interest rate risk perspective of how the intent change is consistent with their overall risk management policies and procedures.

If a bank enters into a commitment with the intention to hold the funded loan for sale, it should account for that commitment under Alternative A or Alternative B described above. If the bank subsequently changes its assertion to an intent to hold a loan for investment, it should continue to consistently apply its previously selected accounting alternative through the date that its intent changed, including recording any loss that would be required under Alternative A or B immediately prior to the change in intent; the bank should not reverse any prior loss recognized under selected method.

Loans Held for Investment

AICPA Statement of Position 01-6, "Accounting by Certain Entities that Lend to or Finance the Activities of Others" (SOP 01-6) states that non-mortgage loans should only be accounted for as held for investment if "management has the intent and ability to hold for the foreseeable future or until maturity or payoff." Loans classified as held for investment are initially recorded at their unpaid principal balance net of discounts, premiums, nonrefundable fees and costs. Following the guidance in FAS 91, "Accounting for Nonrefundable Fees and Costs Associated with Originating or Acquiring Loans and Initial Direct Costs of Leases," nonrefundable fees and costs should be deferred and amortized over the life of the loans as an adjustment to yield. Finally, loans classified as held for investment must be evaluated for impairment following the guidance, as appropriate, in either FAS 5 or FAS 114, "Accounting by Creditors for Impairment of a Loan," as amended and in accordance with the OCC Bulletin 2001- 37, "Policy Statement on Allowance for Loan and Lease Losses Methodologies and Documentation for Banks and Savings Institutions," and OCC Bulletin 2006-47, "Allowance for Loan and Lease Losses."

Loans Held for Sale

Banks must account for loans held for sale under one of the following methods: fair value under the fair value option (FAS 159), the lower of cost or market value (LOCOM) under SOP 01-6, or as the hedged item in a hedge qualifying for fair value hedge accounting under FAS 133, "Accounting for Derivative Instruments and Hedging Activities." Each reporting period, banks must calculate the fair value of their held for sale loans following the guidance for fair value measurement in FAS 157. The accounting for value changes will vary depending on whether the bank elects LOCOM accounting, FAS 133 hedge accounting, or the fair value option (FAS 159).

For loans accounted for at LOCOM, the carrying amount should be adjusted through a valuation allowance (if the fair value is less than carrying amount) with changes in the valuation allowance reported in earnings. In contrast, if the bank hedges the loans and qualifies for fair value hedge accounting pursuant to FAS 133, the bank will adjust the carrying amount of the hedged loans, through earnings, to reflect the change in fair value that is attributable to the hedged risk.

As noted previously, under the fair value option (FAS 159), all changes in the fair value of the loan will adjust the carrying amount and be reflected in current period earnings.

Transfers from Held for Sale to Held for Investment

If a bank decides not to sell a loan after recording the loan at the lower of cost or fair value under held for sale accounting, the loan is transferred to the held for investment category at the current carrying value of the loan (that is, at the lower of cost or fair value.) The transfer date is important, as the lower of cost or fair value on that date is used to establish a new cost basis for that loan. After the transfer into the portfolio, the loan should be evaluated in accordance with the bank's normal credit policies for purposes of establishing an allowance for loan losses related to any probable losses that are incurred after the transfer.

As noted earlier, for loans accounted for as held for investment, management has the intent and ability to hold for the foreseeable future or until maturity or payoff. Consequently, the bank must document it now has the positive intent and ability to hold the loans for the foreseeable future or until maturity. A bank changing its intention and selling the loan(s) or transferring the loan(s) back to the held for sale portfolio would likely cause increased skepticism and scrutiny by the auditor and examiner, especially if the sale occurred during the period the bank originally considered its foreseeable future.

Transfers from Held for Investment to Held for Sale

A bank should transfer loans from the held for investment category to the held for sale category when it no longer has the intent and ability to hold the loans for the foreseeable future or until maturity or payoff. See OCC Bulletin 2001-15, "Loans Held for Sale," for further guidance on these transfers.

Leveraged Lending References

Comptroller's Handbook

"Community Bank Supervision," July 2004

"Large Bank Supervision," May 2001

OCC Issuances

Advisory Letter 99-4, "Leveraged Lending"

Banking Circular 181, "Purchases of Loans In Whole or In Part-Participations, August 2, 1984

Examining Circular 245, "Highly Leveraged Transactions," December 14, 1988

OCC Bulletin 2001-15, "Loans Held for Sale," March 26, 2001

OCC Bulletin 2001-18, "Leverage Finance – Sound Risk Management Practices," April 9, 2001

OCC Bulletin 2001- 37, "Policy Statement on Allowance for Loan and Lease Losses Methodologies and Documentation for Banks and Savings Institutions"

OCC Bulletin 2006-47, "Allowance for Loan and Lease Losses"

OCC Bulletin 2007-1, "Complex Structured Finance Transaction"